The Queen's Coronation Day

THE PICTORIAL RECORD
OF THE GREAT OCCASION

With The Eye-Witness Story of Her Majesty's Crowning

By BEVERLEY NICHOLS

A TINY FIGURE, she seems, frail and feminine, yet invested with an aura of indescribable majesty, for now at last she is Queen indeed.

A figure from a fairy-tale, sending a little smile to her six women of the bedchamber, walking slowly towards us from the altar, her head held high under the glittering crown, wearing her Robe of State which the heralds call purple, though to me it has the colour of deep-dyed violets after rain.

A figure poised at the climax of a supreme moment in history, with all the emblems of Church and State about her—the Sceptre with the Cross in her right hand, the Orb in her left. This is the same Orb which the Archbishop of Canterbury had delivered to her, earlier in the service, with the words . . .

Receive this Orb set under the Cross, and remember that the whole world is subject to the Power and Empire of Christ our Redeemer.

How it sparkles, that Orb, as she draws closer to us, while the organ roars, and the vast congregation sings "God Save the Queen!" How it glows and glitters in the light of the chandeliers, whose brilliance is made the more vivid by the storm clouds massing in the sky outside.

Behind her, her six maids of honour, in dresses of a white so dazzling, so richly sewn with golden sequins, that the effect is of sun-

One of the first pictures of the newly-crowned Queen

★   ★   ★

light sparkling upon snow, and then the Mistress of the Robes, the Dowager Duchess of Devonshire, with a long train of crimson velvet.

Continued on page 5

THE START OF THE GREAT DAY

ABOVE: They don't care if it rains, how chill the wind blow
or even if it snows! They've been there all night. More th
130,000 'camped out' on the pavements along the route
the procession for the whole night before Coronation D
A scene in Northumberland Avenue. LEFT: You can't m
an inch, even seven or eight hours before the procession arriv
An early morning picture in Trafalgar Square. BELOW, le
Overnight the priceless Coronation Regalia has lain un
guard in the Abbey. Now the Canons carry it in process
through the Cloisters—first the Chalice, next the Great Bi
then the Imperial State Crown. BELOW, right: The Dean
Westminster, The Very Rev. Alan C. Don, carries St. Edwar
Crown on a crimson cushion.

THE PRIME MINISTER LEAVES FOR THE ABBEY

ABOVE, *left*: The Prime Minister, Sir Winston Churchill, leaves 10, Downing Street. His grandchildren see him off. From his chain depends the Great George, huge badge of the Order of the Garter, which belonged to his famous ancestor, the 1st Duke of Marlborough. *Centre*: Lady Churchill wears satin and a glittering tiara. *Right*: Peers and Peeresses queue at the Abbey. BELOW: The Lord Mayor of London, Sir Rupert De La Bére, drives to Westminster in his golden coach.

THE PROCESSIONS WIND THEIR WAY TO WESTMINSTER

ABOVE: Between sentinel guardsmen and bluejackets, the Commonwealth Prime Ministers ride out in their carriages to Westminster. RIGHT: Princess Alexandra of Kent waves from a carriage in which she travels with her mother and her brothers—Prince Michael, opposite her and, in his robes in the far corner, the Duke of Kent. BELOW, *right:* The Duchess of Gloucester leaves Buckingham Palace, preceded by her sons, Prince William and Prince Richard. BELOW: The Princess Royal, the Queen's aunt, rides with the Duchess of Gloucester.

LEFT : In the Irish State Coach Queen Elizabeth The Queen Mother and Princess Margaret drive on to Victoria Embankment with a Captain's Escort of the Household Cavalry. RIGHT : A close-up of the Queen Mother and Princess Margaret.

WHEN THAT FAIRY-TALE FIGURE APPEARED . . .

And all around her a throng of colour from the Bishops, the Knights of the Garter, the Knights of the Thistle, the Kings of Arms, the Ministers of State, the peers, the peeresses and the pages. Do not ask me to place all these noble personages in their correct order ; at this stage in the proceedings I am too dizzy with colour, too spent with emotion. I can see Viscount Portal in the dark sweeping robes of the Knight of the Garter . . . and near him Viscount Montgomery, turning to his little white-clad page ; I catch a glimpse of the Duchess of Kent, radiant as a gleam of moonlight, and the fair hair of the Duke of Edinburgh, who is smiling.

But the picture is too crowded; one is overwhelmed. I can only give you a series of impressions, as they struck one Englishman, whose heart was so full that at times his eyes were misted.

There were many human touches in the period of waiting. I shall always remember the two princes of Gloucester, sitting in their kilts on each side of their mother, swinging their legs. And how she turned first to one and then to the other, and gently reproved them . . . and how the swinging legs abruptly came to attention !

I shall always remember how generous was the Queen Mother with her smile and bows . . . how she singled out individual friends for her special attention.

Let us go back to the beginning. From the moment when that fairy-tale figure appeared, gliding slowly across the golden carpet, the Queen dominated the day. Not merely because of the material magnificence with which, as the service progressed, she was invested, but because of what I can only describe as an inner radiance.

It is fitting that the first spoken words of the service should come from the Archbishop, and no more dramatic device could have been chosen than the manner in which he speaks them. The Queen is standing by King Edward's Chair. Slowly from the altar walks the Archbishop, in a white cope and mitre richly embroidered in gold. From his shoulders hangs a magnificent stole of gold, with a pattern of the Cross flanked by vine leaves of brilliant green.

In the Archbishop's wake, gravely and with measured step, walk the Lord Chancellor, the Lord Great Chamberlain, the Lord High Constable, and the Earl Marshal,

Continued on page 15

ABOVE: The Queen's Progress to the ancient Abbey is under way. Her Majesty's guardsmen, airmen and sailors line the route. BELOW, *left*: The wonderful precision of the procession is seen from this bird's-eye view as it passes down The Mall towards Admiralty Arch. BELOW: The Queen reaches Trafalgar Square.

ABOVE: "Oh, lo-ook!" Prince Charles points as, from a window in Buckingham Palace, he and his sister, Princess Anne, watch the crowds gathered along the Mall—down which the Queen, their mother, with the Duke of Edinburgh, their father, are about to leave in the golden State Coach on the Royal Progress to the Abbey.

A CORONATION DAY SMILE FROM THE QUEEN

" How happy the Queen looks! " That was what her people were saying throughout this historic day as they cheered her on
her triumphal Coronation drive. Beside her the Duke of Edinburgh wears the full dress uniform of an Admiral of the Fleet

THE QUEEN ALIGHTS AT THE ABBEY

Big Ben strikes 11 o-clock. Our radiant Sovereign Lady arrives at the Abbey following her 35-minute drive, amid tumultuous acclaim, from the Palace. The Duke of Edinburgh watches anxiously as three of the Queen's maids of honour, assisted by members of her coach team, lift her long train clear of the ground.

THE ROYAL PROCESSIONS IN THE ABBEY

Beautifully begowned, the Royal Ladies walk to the Royal Gallery. ABOVE: The Duchess of Kent's procession. BELOW, *left:* Th
Princess Margaret. Her white dress is embroidered in pearl and silver. BELOW, *right:* The Queen Mother. Ostrich feathers ar
embroidered on her white satin gown in gold, silver and crystal.

THE QUEEN'S FIRST PROGRESS ALONG THE NAVE

As the choir sings the lovely anthem " I was glad when they said unto me . . ." the Queen and her entourage proceed along the Nave of the Abbey towards the Theatre. On either side are her Supporting Bishops, the Bishop of Bath and Wells (on her left), and the Bishop of Durham. The holders of these bishoprics have fulfilled this joint role since the time of Richard I.

THE QUEEN ARRIVES IN THE THEATRE

ABOVE: The nob[le] drama of the crow[n]ing is about [to] commence. Th[e] Queen is now in th[e] Theatre, scene of th[e] Coronation ritua[l] for nigh on [a] thousand years.

★ ★ ★

THE SCENE IS S[ET]

LEFT: Her Majes[ty] takes her seat in t[he] Chair of Estate. H[er] long crimson tra[in] trails on the go[ld] carpet. In the Roy[al] Gallery, her moth[er] and her sist[er] Princess Marga[ret] with her aunt, [the] Princess Royal, a[nd] other members [of] the Royal fam[ily] look down. Beh[ind] the Queen is [the] Abbey's gold pla[te].

The Recognition. ABOVE, *left*: The Queen just before the Recognition Ceremony. The Archbishop is about to present to the people " Queen Elizabeth, your undoubted Queen." Back from the Abbey's vast congregation comes the mighty shout " God Save Queen Elizabeth ! " ABOVE: The Queen signs the Oath after promising to govern her Peoples according to their laws and to maintain the Protestant religion.

RIGHT: " Here is Wisdom . . . these are the lively Oracles of God." The Moderator of the General Assembly of the Church of Scotland, the Rev. Pitt Watson, presents the Holy Bible to the Queen. BELOW : The Bible

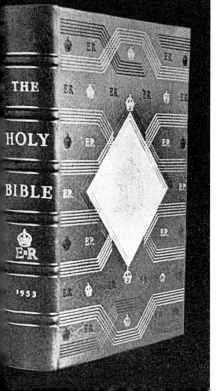

THE ANOINTING

The Queen, divested of her robes, sits in King Edward's Chair for the Anointing, the most mystical part of the Coronation ritual, by which she is held to be imbued with grace. Four Knights of the Garter hold over her a canopy of golden cloth to screen her from the general view during this sacred office. The Archbishop anoints her with holy oil on hand, breast and forehead.

" QUEEN ELIZABETH YOUR UNDOUBTED QUEEN "

preceded by Garter King of Arms, the Hon. Sir George Bellew.   Here is a procession rich in gold and crimson, flanked by the paler shades of the attendant pages, in white and lavender and primrose yellow.   But perhaps the most striking figure, at this moment, is that of the Lord Chancellor, in sombre black heavily slashed with gold, his head surmounted by a majestic wig that seems to symbolize all the dignity of the Law.

The Archbishop halts his steps.   He is now facing the East.   He raises his head, and calls out in a clear voice:

Sirs, I here present unto you Queen Elizabeth, your undoubted Queen: Wherefore all you who are come this day to do your homage and service, Are you willing to do the same ?

The little figure turns towards us.

Whereupon, with one voice we cry:

GOD SAVE QUEEN ELIZABETH!

It is like a rumble of thunder, this acclamation, but there is sweetness in it as well . . .

Continued on page 20.

PRESENTED WITH THE SOVEREIGN'S SWORD

ABOVE: The Queen holds the Sovereign's Sword while the Archbishop, reading from the Coronation rubric, exhorts her to use it " to stop the growth of iniquity, protect the Holy Church of God and defend widows and orphans . . ." BELOW: The Archbishop delivers into the Queen's right hand the Orb, signifying the domination of Christ over the whole world.

Prince Charles, in the Royal Gallery, seems awestruck by the magnificence of the Abbey ceremony.

One of the unforgettable pictures of the unforgettable day! Our Sovereign Lady rides to her Coronation in the State Coach which was built in 1762 to the design of Sir William Chambers. The coach has borne seven Sovereigns to Westminster Abbey for their crowning, George IV, William IV, Victoria, Edward VII, George V, George VI, and Her Majesty Queen Elizabeth II.

H.M. QUEEN ELIZABETH II IS CROWNED

" O God . . . bless this Crown, and so sanctify thy servant Elizabeth . . . that she may be filled by thine abundant grace with all princely virtues." The Archbishop takes up St. Edward's Crown and places it upon the Queen's head. Queen Elizabeth II is crowned. In her right hand is the Sceptre with the Cross, ensign of power and justice, and in her left the Rod with the Dove, symbol of equity and mercy.

—AND NOW THE ENTHRONING

RIGHT: The Duke of Edinburgh and the Duke of Gloucester watch a superb scene in the Abbey, while the Duke of Kent studies his book of the service. BELOW: Now comes the time of the Queen's Enthronement. Wearing St. Edward's Crown, carrying the Sceptre and the Rod with the Dove, she paces slowly towards the steps leading to the Throne in which she is to be "lifted" (actually she is assisted) by Archbishops, Bishops and other Peers. Grouped around the Throne are the Great Officers of State and the Nobles who carried the regalia.

The Queen has been " lifted " into the Throne and as she sits holding the Sceptre and the Rod with the Dove, the Archbishop reads the exhortation: " Stand firm, and hold fast from henceforth the seat and state of Royal and imperial dignity."

THE FABULOUS RUBY OF THE BLACK PRINCE

the sweetness of women's voices. Before our cries have died away, the trumpets sound, in one of those soaring, vibrating fanfares which punctuate so many of the more poignant interludes of the service. Never, I think, has there been such breath-taking music as the music of these trumpets. They are challenging and triumphant; they hold a thousand echoes, echoes of history, that stretch far back into the past, to the field of Agincourt itself . . . that same Agincourt where Henry V won immortal spurs. And while he was winning them, there shone in his helmet the fabulous ruby of the Black Prince . . . that same ruby which, at this very moment, is set in the Imperial State Crown, the crown which will soon be set on the head of the slender figure standing by King Edward's Chair.

Four times the Archbishop demands the Recognition, to the East, to the South, to the West, and to the North, and each time that he does so the Queen turns to us. And there echoes back to her the cry " *God Save Queen Elizabeth!* "

I am trying to make you feel that you are here in the Abbey with me. I want you to see not only a static picture in colour, however vivid, but a picture that actually moves and lives. Therefore, as we watch, I must emphasize that this procession—and indeed, nearly all the processions that are to follow it—takes place in slow motion. There are few hurried footsteps or speedy gestures. Even the pages, as they go about their various duties, do so in a boyish edition of a slow march. In terms of music, the tempo is *lento*. But it is *lento non troppo* . . . slow, but not too slow . . . for after the first few moments you come to accept this rhythm as the natural rhythm of life; it is as though Father Time,

Continued on page 22

HER HUSBAND'S HOMAGE

The Duke of Edinburgh pays homage to the Queen, his wife. He kneels before her, places his hands between hers and pronounces his homage in the traditional words of the rubric " I Philip, Duke of Edinburgh, do become your liege man of life and limb . . . to live and die, against all manner of folks . . . " He rises and, bending, touches the Queen's crown and kisses her on the left cheek.

THE CELEBRATION OF HOLY COMMUNION

ABOVE: The Queen and the Duke of Edinburgh kneel together at Holy Communion in front of the High Altar after the rites of the Coronation itself are ended. The Queen has given up her Crown and kneels, bareheaded, on a faldstool. BELOW: The two-hour service is over and the newly-crowned Queen leaves the Theatre in the Great Procession on the way to the West Door.

FOR THE FIRST TIME WE HEAR THE QUEEN'S VOICE

in the Abbey, had halted in his tracks, and put away his scythe, impelled by an overwhelming sense of reverence and of awe.

Now comes the Oath, and for the first time we hear the Queen's voice. She has returned to her chair and the Archbishop stands in front of her.

" Madam, is your Majesty willing to take the Oath ? "

" I am willing " she replies. Her voice is so low, so reverent, that perhaps it is only in our fancy that we hear it at all. But her next response, when she solemnly promises to govern her wide-spread dominions according to their laws and customs, is clearer . . . and grows in strength till the final " So help me God," which she speaks at the altar, on her knees, with her maids of honour kneeling behind her.

She kisses the Book, signs the Oath, and again returns to her chair. Now is the moment when England and Scotland give proof of their spiritual unity. We see the tall, spare figure of the Dean of Westminster, in a cope of deepest red, handing the Bible to the Moderator of the General Assembly of the Church of Scotland. And we hear the Moderator saying the magical words " Here is Wisdom: This is the royal Law: These are the lively Oracles of God."

Sight or sound . . . it would be difficult to say by which of the senses we are most enraptured. For as the Queen kneels, and the Communion service begins, we hear softly, as from a great distance, the opening phrases of Howells' anthem " Behold, O God, Our Defender." That is one thing you must never forget, if you wish to gain a true impression of this ceremony; its constant interludes of exquisite music. And another thing you must not forget—paradoxical as it may seem —is the *silence* with which the figures move. One usually associates the Abbey—or indeed, any church in the land—with footsteps echoing over the marble pavements, with a subdued but definite clatter. Today all this is hushed by the deep golden carpet over which the pageant moves. This hush adds immensely to the drama of the occasion.

Continued on page 24.

THE QUEEN GOES OUT TO HER PEOPLE

In St. Edward's Chapel the Queen has been arrayed in her Purple Robe of State. Wearing the Imperial State Crown and with the long train of the Robe borne by her maids of honour, Her Majesty joins the Great Procession out of the Abbey to where the expectant crowds are waiting for the coming of their newly crowned Queen. The organ peals out and the voices of the vast congregation break forth together into the singing of " God Save The Queen."

THE "RADIANT WHITENESS" OF THE QUEEN

And drama it is indeed, from now onwards, for in a succession of mounting climax come the Anointing, the Presenting of the Spurs and Sword, the Investing with the Armills, the Stole Royal and the Robe Royal, and the Putting on of the Crown itself. It would be impossible to describe in detail so complex a pattern of ceremony, each moment of which is filled with spiritual and historical significance. I can only paint a few fragmentary pictures which seemed to me of special beauty.

Firstly, the sudden radiant whiteness of the Queen as she was divested of her glowing crimson robe, before the Anointing, and the lovely movements of her maids, as they reverently handed it to the Lord Great Chamberlain.

Then, the pomp and majesty of the procession in which the four Knights of the Garter advanced with the pall of cloth of gold, which they held over her head during the Anointing. This pall, which must be of very great weight, seemed almost luminous as they set it over the throne.

Again, the intense stillness in the Abbey as the Archbishop leant over the Queen, saying . . . Be thy Hands anointed with holy Oil, Be thy Breast anointed with holy Oil, be thy Head anointed with holy Oil . . . " a stillness that was all the more impressive because it came immediately in the wake of the Allelujahs that end Handel's triumphant anthem Zadok the Priest.

And then, the brilliant flash of jewels as the Archbishop lays on the altar the Sword of State.

But this brilliance is as nothing to the sudden blaze of gold which dazzles us when

★ ★ ★

ROYAL EXIT FROM THE ABBEY

ABOVE, *left : A close-up of the Queen walking in the Great Procession out of the Abbey, showing the Royal Cipher E II R below the Crown on the train of her Purple Robe of State.* BELOW, *left : The Duke of Edinburgh in ermine-topped robe and coronet walks behind the Heralds in their medieval tabards and white silken breeches and silken hose.*

the Queen is invested with the Armills and clad in the Robe Royal. This is of a gold so startling that for a moment it seems to turn the Queen into a statue of precious metal.

Even this is surpassed by the supreme moment of the Putting on of the Crown. Try to imagine this . . . the Archbishop slowly advancing from the altar, flanked by his attendant bishops, St. Edward's Crown glittering against the scarlet vestments of the Dean who is holding it, the statuesque golden figure of the Queen herself, sitting in King Edward's Chair. And then . . . a sudden gesture of the Archbishop, as he boldly holds the Crown aloft, and lowers it on to the Queen's head. It is the signal for an outburst of sound and of movement. The rafters ring as we shout *God Save The Queen*, and there is a flurry of crimson and ermine as the Princesses, the Peers and Peeresses put on their coronets and caps, and the Kings of Arms their crowns.

All London, one feels, must hear the fanfare of trumpets which acclaims this moment, just as all London must hear the distant rumble of the guns of the Tower.

It would seem impossible, after the act of the Putting on of the Crown, that the sense of climax should continue, let alone that it should be enhanced. But history is a great dramatist, and it is by history that this superb liturgy has been written. The directions in the service now state that the Queen, being enthroned . . . " all the Great Officers, those that bear the Swords and the Sceptres, and the Nobles who carried the other Regalia, *shall stand round about the steps of the Throne*." What happens, in fact, is that they stand *on* the steps, grouped behind it with their rich cloaks falling over the dais, so that the effect is one of a dazzling arch of colour.

Now, from his standpoint in the North Transept, a little page in white walks slowly across the great empty space, bearing in his hands a crimson cushion. Drama again! There is something strangely touching in the sight of this small figure, on whom the spotlight of history has momentarily rested. In fact, he is Duncan Davidson, nephew of the Earl Marshal, and his function—after he ascended the steps and knelt before the Queen —is to remain on the left of the throne, receiving the coronets of those who come to do their obeisance. Very gracefully, we

Continued on page 26

ABOVE : The Queen Mother's train is carried by her four pages as she precedes Princess Margaret from the Abbey. BELOW : Carrying Sceptre and Orb, the Queen is again seen outside the Abbey, about to enter her coach and start the five-mile drive back to the Palace through cheering masses of her subjects who, despite the rain, have waited proudly and patiently.

THE DUKE OF EDINBURGH
DOES HIS HOMAGE

notice, he receives them, standing at strict attention, inclining his small head with old world courtesy as each of the nobles places his coronet on the cushion.

Now comes the moment for which every woman in the Abbey has been waiting, the moment when the Duke of Edinburgh comes forward to do his homage. For the first time in the service, I hear a faint but distinct whisper from the congregation, like a breeze blowing down the Abbey, a whisper from a thousand feminine lips. And well might the women whisper, for if the Queen is a Faery Queen, here indeed is her Faery Prince. The lights gleam on his fair hair as he strides forward, and we notice that his pace is quicker than the rest, as though he were eager to kneel at the feet of the woman he loves.

Dead silence. He places his hands between hers, and these are the words he repeats:

I Philip, Duke of Edinburgh, do become your liege man of life and limb, and of earthly worship: and faith and truth I will bear unto you, to live and die, against all manner of folks. So help me God.

And then one of the most touching moments in the whole ceremony when he rises, touches her crown and kisses her cheek. Very gently, but very proudly.

When the Homage is ended there is a mighty roll of drums, and a swift fanfare of trumpets. At last, all the pent-up emotions of the great congregation have a chance of release. For this is where we are allowed to shout . . .

God Save Queen Elizabeth
Long Live Queen Elizabeth
May the Queen live for ever !

And shout we do, though there are many who find that their voices have grown husky, and that there is a suspicious mist before their eyes. The little figure whom we are acclaiming is so frail, so mortal; there is not a man here, at this moment—if indeed he is a man—who would not feel honoured to risk his very life, to save her from harm.

The picture of the day. Thousands saw the Queen like this. Many others will also treasure this human photograph of the radiant Sovereign, so obviously happy as she rides triumphantly " home " to Buckingham Palace.

★ ★ ★

Hardly have the echoes of our voices died away than the organ swells out in that most joyous and comforting of hymns " All people that on earth do dwell." The whole Abbey joins in, and it is to this roar of voices and of organ music that the Queen walks slowly down the steps of the throne, supported and attended as before. Gently . . . almost hesitantly . . . she hands St. Edward's crown to the Lord Great Chamberlain, and her Sceptre and Rod. There is a moment's pause. Then she clasps her hands, and raises her head, and kneels at the altar.

So natural is her piety, so deep her devotion, that I am reminded of a young girl kneeling at her bedside to say her simple prayers.

Continued on page 28

THE RETURN TO THE PALACE

Top, left: A roar of cheering goes up from the thousands massed about the Abbey as the State Coach, reflected in the rain-washed road, is pulled away on the long road back to the Palace. Troops from every part of the Commonwealth have now joined the procession: from Australia and New Zealand, from Pakistan, from the British Solomon Islands and the remote Falklands. ABOVE, right: Pipers of the Gurkhas Brigade and the Pakistan Army pass through the Marble Arch. RIGHT: The British Grenadiers! A detachment of the Footguards—of which the Queen is Colonel-in-Chief—swing rhythmically into Pall Mall.

A YOUNG CHRISTIAN QUEEN AND HER HUSBAND . . .

But meanwhile the pomp and pageantry continues . . . and the music. Never forget that music, if you wish to share this historic moment! We have come to the last verse . . . .

To Father, Son, and Holy Ghost
The God whom heaven and earth adore
From men and from the Angel-host
Be praise and glory evermore.

The organ is full *crescendo*—and so are we! After each line there is a pause, and a fanfare of trumpets. The effect is indescribably thrilling. For these fanfares are not just musical decorations . . . they are like swift choruses of acclamation; they stir the blood and exalt the spirit.

We are nearing the end of the pageantry; the fanfares cease and their echoes die away; the Communion Service continues . . . that service beside which even the Coronation itself seems but a pale shadow. It is not for me to attempt to describe it, not to note the colours and movements which attend it. It is enough to know that a young Christian Queen and her husband are kneeling there at the altar, before the great ones of the Earth, paying their homage to the Son of God. These are not things that can be said in words, though they may be hinted in music. And it is one of the triumphs of the Coronation that when all words are inadequate, the ceremony turns to song.

The Archbishop is at the Lord's Table. His voice gains power as he intones:

Therefore with Angels and Archangels, and
with all the company of heaven, we laud and
magnify thy glorious Name: evermore
praising thee, and saying . . .

The next words, of course, are Holy, Holy, Holy. But they do not come from the lips of the Archbishop; they drift down to us, in a high, sweet whisper, from the choir aloft. Or as it seems to us, kneeling there, from heaven itself; for if ever there was music worthy of being called sacred, it is this. It is taken from the Communion Service in G minor, which is one of the most truly inspired works of that grand old British composer, Vaughan Williams. The treble voices drift in thirds, in a series of exquisite cadences . . . it is as though there were bird-song in the rafters.

They have made their Communion. They rise, and the vast congregation rises with them. " Glory be to God on high " we sing, with a sense of triumph and exaltation. It seems natural that we kneel again, to hear the Archbishop invoke for us " the Peace of God which passeth all understanding." And it seems not only natural but inevitable that we should rise for the last time, for the *Te Deum.* This anthem, set to music by Sir William Walton, is truly inspired.

My pen has run dry. There are no more colours in it . . . no more of the scarlets and purples and crimsons in which such a story should be told. Only one last single drop of gold, with which to write Full Stop.

But it needs no colour to write the final words . . . nothing but printer's ink.

★　　　★　　　★

GOD SAVE THE QUEEN !

THE BALCONY SCENE

ABOVE: The spectacle witnessed by the vast crowds that massed in front of the Palace after the Queen's return. Between the Queen and her husband stand their children, the Duke of Cornwall and Princess Anne. Prince Charles wears his first medal—the Silver Coronation medal. There, too, are the Queen Mother and Princess Margaret. On the right of the picture is the Duchess of Kent and her family, and the two Princes of Gloucester. On the left is the Duchess of Gloucester. RIGHT: Here comes the R.A.F. ! The airman-Duke was the first to detect the whine of the jet engines (he is seen looking up from the balcony in the picture above). This was the R.A.F.'s Coronation salute to the Queen. 168 aircraft took part but they had to use open formation since bad weather made it too risky to fly wing-tip to wing-tip. BELOW: Prince Charles points excitedly while the Queen and the whole of the balcony party look up.

HER MAJESTY'S
CORONATION SPEECH

Below is the text of the Queen's speech, which was broadcast at 9 p.m. on her Coronation Day, 2nd June, 1953.

WHEN I spoke to you last, at Christmas, I asked you all whatever your religion, to pray for me on the Day of my Coronation.

To pray that God would give me wisdom and strength to carry out the promises that I should then be making. Throughout this memorable day I have been uplifted and sustained by the knowledge that your thoughts and prayers were with me.

I have been aware all the time that my peoples spread far and wide throughout every Continent and Ocean in the world were united to support me in the task to which I have now been dedicated with such solemnity.

Many thousands of you came to London from all parts of the Commonwealth and Empire to join in the Ceremony, but I have been conscious, too, of the millions of others who have shared in it by means of wireless or television in their homes. All of you, near, or far, have been united in one purpose. It is hard for me to find words in which to tell you of the strength which this knowledge has given me.

The Ceremonies you have seen today are ancient and some of their origins are veiled in the mysteries of the past, but their spirit and their meaning shine through the Ages, never, perhaps, more brightly than now. I have in sincerity pledged myself to your service, as so many of you are pledged to mine. Throughout all my life and with all my heart I shall strive to be worthy of your trust.

In this resolve, I have my husband to support me. He shares all my ideals and all my affection for you. Then, although my experience is so short and my task so new, I have in my parents and grand-parents an example which I can follow with certainty, and with confidence. There is also this. I have behind me not only the splendid traditions and the annals of more than a thousand years, but the living strength and majesty of the Commonwealth and Empire. Of societies old and new, of lands and races different in history and origins, but all by God's Will united in spirit and in aim.

Therefore, I am sure that this, my Coronation, is not the symbol of a power and a splendour that are gone, but a declaration of our hopes for the future and for the years I may, by God's grace and mercy be given to reign and serve you as your Queen.

I have been speaking of the vast regions and varied peoples to whom I owe my duty, but there has also sprung from our island home a theme of social and political thought which constitutes our message to the world and through the changing generations has found acceptance both within and far beyond my realms. Parliamentary institutions, with their free speech and respect for the rights of minorities, and the inspiration of a broad tolerance in thought and

On her return to Buckingham Palace from the State Processions through London, Her Majesty posed for this official portrait.

★ ★ ★

its expression. All this we conceive to be a precious part of our way of life and outlook.

During recent centuries this message has been sustained and invigorated by the immense contribution in language, literature and action of the nations of our Commonwealth overseas. It gives expression as I pray it always will, to living principles as sacred to the Crown and monarchy as to its many Parliaments and Peoples.

I ask you now to cherish them and practise them too, then we can go forward together in peace, seeking justice and freedom for all men.

As this day draws to its close, I know that my abiding memory of it will be not only the solemnity and beauty of the Ceremony but the inspiration of your loyalty and affection.

I thank you all from a full heart.

God bless you all.

QUEEN AND CONSORT

The Queen and the Duke. An official picture taken in the Throne Room at Buckingham Palace. The Queen's magnificent Coronation dress, the details of which were kept a secret from the public until Coronation Day, is seen in all its beauty. On her wrists the Queen wears the Armills, the gold " bracelets of sincerity and wisdom " presented to her by the Commonwealth.

THE QUEEN SWITCHES ON LONDON'S LIGHTS

ABOVE : Family group at Buckingham Palace. Prince Charles looks smart in his long white trousers, Princess Anne pretty in her white frock. LEFT : The floodlit Mall. And it was the Queen herself who, pressing a switch at the Palace, set the famous way ablaze with lights, the signal in its turn for a rippling wave of brilliance to flash all round the capital. There are perhaps 150,000 people in the Mall and the other approaches to the Palace. BELOW : The Queen and the Duke, picked out by the lights, wave from the balcony to the wildly cheering multitude.